East Jackson Elementary
Media Center
1531 Hoods Mill Rd
Commerce, GA 30529

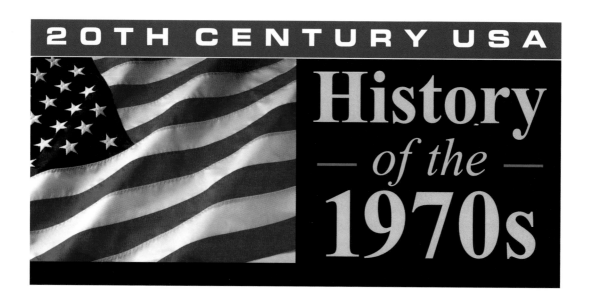

20TH CENTURY USA

History of the 1970s

Rennay Craats

WEIGL PUBLISHERS INC.

Published by Weigl Publishers Inc.
123 South Broad Street, Box 227
Mankato, MN, USA
Web site: http://www.weigl.com

Library of Congress Cataloging-in-Publication Data available upon request
from the publisher. Fax (507) 388-2746 for the attention of the Publishing
Records Department.

ISBN 1-930954-34-4

Printed and bound in the United States of America
1 2 3 4 5 6 7 8 9 0   05 04 03 02 01

Senior Editor
Jared Keen

Series Editor
Carlotta Lemieux

Copy Editor
Heather Kissock

Layout and Design
Warren Clark
Carla Pelky

Photo Research
Joe Nelson

Photograph Credits

Archive Photos: pages 3MR, 6BR, 19T, 19B, 20, 23, 27B, 35, 38, 42; Bettmann/CORBIS:
pages 22, 28; Ed Carlin/Archive Photos: page 34; CORBIS: pages 7BR, 8; Rennay Craats:
page 27T; Meaghan Craven: page 37B; Kent State University: page 9B; Lyn McAfee/Archive
Photos: page 40; NASA: pages 6BRL, 26; National Archives of Canada: page 14; New
York Times Co./Angel Franco/Archive Photos: pages 3B, 24; New York Times Co./Tyrone
Dukes/Archive Photos: page 25; Photofest: pages 3ML, 7BL, 10, 11, 12, 13, 15, 29, 30, 31,
36, 37T, 41; Reuters NewMedia Inc./CORBIS: page 43; Reuters/Jose Agurto/Archive Photos:
page 17; William L. Rukeyser/Archive Photos: page 18; Russel Reif/Archive Photos: page 32;
Alon Reininger/Archive Photos: page 33; Jim Wells/Archive Photos: page 21.

USA 1970s Contents

Entertainment 10

Literature 24

Immigration 38

Famine in Africa

Disco Fever

Olympic Massacre

WATERGATE

Nixon Resigns

Bicentennial Bash

The King is Dead

Women's Rights

Oil Crisis

Peace in the Middle East

The seventies were a time of social and political change. The feminist movement was making huge strides, students were speaking out against injustice, and governments were being held accountable. An air of activism could be felt throughout many aspects of day-to-day life in the U.S.

The nation gaped at headlines that said President Nixon, who was supposed to lead by example, was facing **impeachment** after the Watergate scandal. Americans felt betrayed by the government.

Nixon's successor, Gerald Ford, survived two assassination attempts within a few weeks of

each other. The U.S. economy faltered as inflation skyrocketed and unemployment rates rose.

Other headlines were bittersweet. The Vietnam War was finally over, and Americans could rebuild their lives with returning soldiers and mourn those lost in the conflict. The Super Bowl champions,

Burundi Civil War

Three Mile Island

CARTER'S AMERICA

Pinochet's Rule

Sophie's Choice

Ingenious Discovery

Panama Controls Canal

ASHE ON FIRE

Brain Drain

the Miami Dolphins, became the first team to finish an entire season undefeated. American ingenuity created the tallest building in the world at the time, the Sears Tower.

20th Century USA: History of the 1970s presents a selection of events that made headlines in this pivotal decade. The stories highlighted here touch on many aspects of U.S. life—from sports and entertainment to politics and immigration. They represent significant moments in the country's history—moments that helped shape the American identity.

To find out more about Watergate, disco, or *Apollo 13*, the library is a great place to start your search. Many newspapers and magazines from the seventies are saved on microfilm. The Internet and encyclopedias are also helpful guides. For now, turn the page, and "dig" the stories of this "far-out" decade.

Time Line

1970

"Okay, Houston, we've had a problem." The *Apollo 13* space mission nearly ends in tragedy when an oxygen tank explodes. Turn to page 26 to find out what happened.

1970

Four people die during a demonstration for peace. Read more about Kent State University on page 9.

1970

Women take to the streets for equality. Marches and rallies fight for women's rights. Turn to page 32 to learn more about the feminist movement.

1971

After twenty years of disagreements, relations between China and the U.S. start to warm up. Find out how on page 42.

1971

Bruce Lee kicks his way to Hollywood. His martial arts and movie sense make him a star. Turn to page 13 to find out what became of the Green Hornet.

1972

Underworld mob families have never been better. See what won Academy Award acclaim on page 10.

1972

The floodgates are opened as Richard Nixon is tied to the Watergate break-in. The country is shocked. Page 21 has more details about the fall of the president.

1972

The Olympic Games are marred by violence. Terrorists break into the Israeli dorms and murder several athletes. Page 30 has the story of this tragedy.

1972

War erupts between Hutus and Tutsis in Burundi. To learn what caused the conflict, turn to page 16.

1973

Chile has a new leader, like it or not. General Pinochet takes the government in a coup and siezes loyalty by force. Turn to page 17 to read about the iron-fisted leader.

1973

Chicago towers over the rest of the world—or at least the Sears Tower does. This structure is recognized as the tallest building in the world at the time. Turn to page 26 to read more.

1974

Mikhail Baryshnikov trades borscht for apple pie. Flip to page 12 to discover more about America's newest Russian ballet dancer.

1974

With one swing of his bat, Hank Aaron becomes part of history. He beats Babe Ruth's home run average. Find out more about this talented baseball player on page 30.

Apollo 13

Gerald Ford

1975

Chinese archeologists unearth thousands of soldiers in Shanxi province. Page 18 has the details about this discovery.

1975

President Gerald Ford's guardian angels are working double-duty in 1975. He is the target of two separate assassination attempts in two weeks. Read more on page 22.

1975

A fight between Muhammad Ali and Joe Frazier is nothing less than a thrill. The "Thrilla in Manila" catches the attention of sixty-five countries around the world. Find out who won this rematch on page 28.

1976

Jimmy Carter enters the White House after a narrow victory over Gerald Ford. Read about his term as president on page 23.

1977

Americans want "The Force" to be with them. They flock to theaters to watch the space battle of good versus evil. Turn to page 11 to see who wins the star wars.

1977

Kennedy Airport goes supersonic! The first supersonic transport takes off from New York in 1977. Page 27 has more details.

1977

The Illegal Alien Task Force takes a look at immigration in the U.S. See what the task force found on page 39.

1977

The King is dead. Millions of fans mourn the death of Elvis Presley in 1977. Is he really gone? Find out on page 41.

1978

John Travolta wows the country and has women feverish with his disco dancing in *Saturday Night Fever*. Read how he helped launch the disco trend on page 15.

1978

How do a construction worker, a leatherman, a police officer, a Native American, a cowboy, and an athlete make it to the top of the music charts? Discover more about these "macho men" on page 40.

1978

According to John Irving, the world is pretty good. His novel about a man named Garp won him awards and fame. Turn to page 25 to read more about this talented writer.

1979

Iranian students take ninety American hostages at the U.S. embassy. They release some, but keep fifty-two of them as bargaining chips. Find out what they wanted and how the crisis ended on page 43.

1979

A leak at a Pennsylvania nuclear waste plant draws serious criticism. The disaster at Three Mile Island could have been worse, but it was bad enough for Americans. Turn to page 8 to learn about the accident.

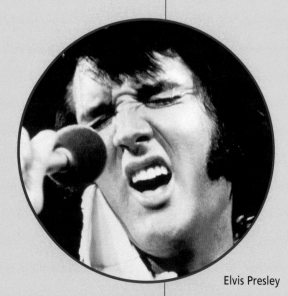

Elvis Presley

Three Mile Island

Three Mile Island

March 28, 1979, marked the worst nuclear disaster in U.S. history. The combination of a stuck valve and a human maintenance error drew international attention to Three Mile Island near Harrisburg, Pennsylvania. A leak within a nuclear power plant released radioactive gases, and authorities were afraid that these gases would explode and cause a **meltdown**. The reactor shut itself down, and the automatic cooling system activated shortly after the leak, but the reactor was heavily contaminated inside, and the accident

caused about $1 billion in damages to the plant.

The fact that only a small amount of gas was released into the air did not make Americans feel better. Residents around the power plant were afraid that next time the leak would be worse,

and people would be harmed. Anti-nuclear activists brought attention to the accident and encouraged Americans to stand up against this energy source before it was too late. Debate continued over nuclear energy.

■ After the Three Mile Island disaster, the Nuclear Regulatory Commission tightened safety regulations.

TROUBLE IN LOVE CANAL

■ Chemicals tainted the Love Canal neighborhood of Niagara Falls, New York, in 1978. In the 1940s and 1950s, the Hooker Chemical Company had dumped its toxic waste into an empty canal. It then filled the canal and sold the land to New York in 1953. Niagara Falls used the land to build houses and schools. Over the following years, complaints of headaches, strange rashes, liver illnesses, birth defects, and several other medical conditions began to surface. No one could pinpoint the cause of the problems until 1976, when heavy rain caused chemical pools to bubble up from the canal into backyards and basements. The area was evacuated, allowing the city to begin an extensive clean-up operation. The costs of the clean up were high, but community residents demanded that it be done.

Niagara Falls was not the only place built on toxic ground. The government guessed that there were more than 1,000 "Love Canals" across the U.S.

Jonestown Tragedy

After the 1960s hippie movement began to disappear, other movements took its place. Religious **cults** promised hope and meaning in people's lives. The Reverend Jim Jones ran church-based services that helped poor and lonely people in California. In 1977, Jones and a few hundred followers left the U.S. to set up a **commune** on a 27,000-acre plot of land in Guyana. He called it Jonestown. Later, some of the followers sent word that people were being beaten, abused, and held captive in the commune.

In 1978, California congressman Leo Ryan and eighteen others flew to the commune to ensure that everything was all right. Jones was friendly at first, but he grew angry. Some of the followers asked Ryan to help them escape, but another attacked the congressman

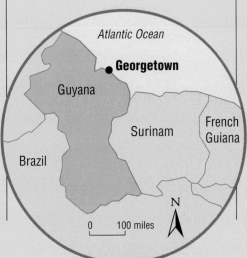

with a knife as he spoke to a couple who were thinking of leaving.

Ryan and his group tried to escape by plane, but he and four others were shot to death. Then Jones called for the ultimate act of loyalty—mass suicide. The Jonestown followers drank a poisoned fruit drink, some willingly and others at gunpoint. Only a few followers escaped. As about 900 people lay dead around him, Jim Jones took his own life with a gun.

▦ Jim Jones was a charismatic leader. Many people believed he was Jesus and followed him to Guyana.

Protesters Silenced with Gunfire

Students from every region of the U.S. protested the country's presence in Cambodia and Vietnam. There were demonstrations on many university campuses, including Ohio's Kent State. On May 4, 1970, the students gathered to voice their opinions. The National Guard was called in, but the students would not leave. The Guard shot tear gas into the crowds, and students responded by throwing rocks. Just after noon, the unthinkable happened. A National Guard commander, who said he heard shots fired, opened fire on the unarmed students. After the smoke cleared, four students were dead and another ten were injured. The

dead were said to be bystanders not actively taking part in the campus demonstrations.

Ten days later, police killed two student protesters at a similar demonstration at Jackson State University in Mississippi. Americans were enraged and saddened by the killings.

▦ Public protests against the U.S. military involvement in Vietnam increased after the violence at Kent State.

Seventy-five U.S. colleges were shut down for the rest of the school year. These shootings prompted many Americans to speak out against the war.

Live From New York

A cast of crazy comedians ruled late-night television in 1975. On October 11, Americans watched *Saturday Night Live* for the first time. It was soon a smash success. Chevy Chase, Jim Belushi, Dan Aykroyd, Jane Curtin, and other talented actors and comedians kept the show fresh and funny. By 1980, all of the original crew had left *Saturday Night Live* to make movies, but new talent took their place. *SNL* continued to entertain television viewers through the years. The stars have included Mike Myers, Dana Carvey, Eddie Murphy, and Molly Shannon.

The hilarious antics of the Saturday Night Live crew continue to make people laugh after more than twenty-five years on the air.

Mafia Draws Theater Crowds

The **mafia** took to the silver screen in 1972. *The Godfather* was about the lives of a powerful mob family, the Corleones, in the 1940s and 1950s. It followed the inner-city war for control over the drug trade between smugglers and the Corleone family. Mario Puzo and Francis Ford Coppola used Puzo's bestselling novel as a base for the screenplay. The film won Academy Awards for best picture and best screenplay. Marlon Brando, who played mafia boss Don Vito Corleone, also earned an Academy Award. Other great actors, including Al Pacino, James Caan, Diane Keaton, and Robert Duvall, helped make the movie a box-office hit—it made $330 million in two-and-a-half years.

The Godfather II was released two years later. It told the story of a young Don Vito Corleone, played by Robert De Niro. The sequel was also a hit, earning six Academy Awards, including one for Best Picture and another for Best Actor, De Niro. The final movie in the **trilogy**, *The Godfather III*, was released in 1990 and followed the crime family's efforts to work on the right side of the law.

JAWS

Just when you thought it was safe to go into the movie theater, there was *Jaws*. The 1975 movie about a violent great white shark was a smash success. It was director Steven Spielberg's first hit. The movie followed an oceanographer, a police officer, and an old sailor as they tried to catch the beast. The film won Academy Awards for sound, editing, and music. The musical theme for *Jaws* terrorized and thrilled moviegoers. Americans flocked to the box office to watch what happened next when *Jaws II* was released in 1978.

Out of This World

In 1977, Americans cheered good over evil as Princess Leia, Han Solo, Luke Skywalker, and a handful of others battled against Darth Vader and his Stormtroopers. *Star Wars* was a huge success at the box office and for the producer, George Lucas, and. The movie earned more than $232 million in North America alone, and it made even more money in theaters around the world. Moviegoers were awed by the incredible special effects, the likes of which had never been seen before. Starships battled each other in space, strange alien life forms interacted, and a robot could be a Jedi fighter's best friend. *Star Wars* won seven Academy Awards, including those for special effects, musical score, art direction, film editing, and costume design. The movie was followed by two sequels, *The Empire Strikes Back* (1980) and *Return of the Jedi* (1983). In 1999, more than twenty years after the original movie hit theaters, Lucas released a **prequel** to *Star Wars* called *The Phantom Menace*.

■ Luke Skywalker, Princes Leia, and Han Solo have appeared in comics, novels, toys, and even video games.

Happy Days Indeed

The U.S. went back to the 1950s in 1974. A new television comedy, *Happy Days*, slowly caught the country's attention. The series enjoyed limited success until the show's writers found their ace in the hole—Arthur Fonzarelli. The Fonz, played by Henry Winkler, was everything cool, with his leather jacket, slangy language, and thumbs-up approval. Once the Fonz's role was increased, the show took off. Americans enjoyed the Fonz and the rest of the Cunningham family until the show came off the air in 1984.

Doonesbury Goes National

Garretson Beekman Trudeau was 21 years old when his comic strip, "Doonesbury," was picked up by newspapers across the country. This political cartoon series featured "real" people in actual situations, including President Nixon and John Mitchell during the Watergate scandal. Trudeau also commented on the U.S. presence in Vietnam, through his regular character B.D. and a North Vietnamese character named Phred the Terrorist. In only five years, "Doonesbury" had developed into a favorite of readers across the nation. It became the only comic strip ever to win the **Pulitzer Prize**. More than 400 newspapers carried the comic strip, and many moved it from the funny pages onto the editorial pages.

Miniseries Takes Root

About half of all Americans turned on their televisions in January 1977. They were **enthralled** with the fictional history of African-American journalist Alex Haley. Haley's bestselling book *Roots* was made into an eight-part miniseries, and it ran every night. Each segment drew an audience of about 80 million viewers. This was the biggest response to a television program ever. *Roots* began with the story of an African who was stolen into slavery in 1750, and it ended seven generations later at an African-American professor's funeral. That professor was Haley's father, and the events Haley relayed came from the stories of his grandmother and her sister. *Roots* won six Emmy Awards, and the novel earned Haley a Pulitzer Prize in 1977.

Although based on a fictional book, the miniseries *Roots* explored more than 200 years of African-American history.

DANCE "MOVES"

The Soviet Union lost its prized dancer on June 24, 1974. Mikhail Baryshnikov was touring Canada with the Bolshoi Ballet when he **defected**—he became one of many talented Russian dancers to leave home for the West. The 26-year-old's dream was to dance with companies around the world, but the Soviet government would not allow it. Baryshnikov was given asylum in Canada. Within a month, the dancer debuted in New York with the American Ballet Theater. He became an instant superstar.

Over the next three years, Baryshnikov performed more than twenty roles. In May 1975, he graced the covers of Time and Newsweek magazines. As well, Baryshnikov received an Academy Award nomination for his role in *The Turning Point* (1977), and was highly acclaimed in the movie *White Nights* (1985). Baryshnikov helped create excitement about ballet in the U.S., and he was a role model for other male dancers.

Make His Day

Americans were ready for a strong cop who would clear their streets of thugs and criminals. Clint Eastwood was happy to meet their needs. In 1971, he made his debut as hot-head Harry Callahan, a San Francisco police detective who was angry about crime. Harry often acted as judge, jury, and executioner when he caught the bad guys. He dared them to try to escape or fight back with his famous phrase "Go ahead, make my day." *Dirty Harry* was a surprise hit with audiences. The low-budget movie made millions at the box office, and it made Clint Eastwood a star. Several other "Dirty" Harry Callahan movies followed through the 1970s and 1980s.

Super Movie

In 1978, the world was finally safe from evil. The blockbuster *Superman* starred Christopher Reeve as the man of steel, Margot Kidder as Lois Lane, and Gene Hackman as the brilliant criminal, Lex Luthor. The film was the revival of the *DC* comic book character Americans had grown up with. Superman was born on the planet Krypton but grew up on an U.S. farm. He became a newspaper reporter by day and a caped crime fighter by night—or by day too if there was trouble. Reeve took his role as the world's strongest man very seriously. He trained to get into superhuman shape, and his body type was noticeably different by the end of the movie. Some of the early scenes had to be reshot so that Superman would look the same throughout. The movie won a special Academy Award for visual effects. It was so popular that three more *Superman* movies were filmed.

"I'm here to fight for truth, justice, and the American way."
Superman to Lois Lane

■ Superman flew from comics to the silver screen. Moviegoers were dazzled by the hero as he soared through the air, lifted tractors, and dodged bullets.

KUNG FU MASTER

■ Chinese American Bruce Lee moved from playing Kato in *The Green Hornet* to being an international star on his own. In 1971, *Fists of Fury* destroyed box-office records throughout Asia. Many people criticized the movie, saying it lacked a plot and meaningful dialogue. Still, Lee stood out as a martial arts wizard as well as an actor. Lee wanted to produce top-notch martial arts films with better moves. *Enter the Dragon* and *Return of the Dragon*, both from 1973, confirmed Lee as a star in this new type of film and brought Hong Kong movies to Western moviegoers. He was the best in the business. His death in 1973 from a **cerebral edema** shocked his fans. Lee's status in the martial arts field remains legendary.

One Flew to the Oscars

The story of a psychiatric hospital caught Oscar fever. *One Flew Over the Cuckoo's Nest* followed Patrick McMurphy, an energetic **anti-hero** played by Jack Nicholson, who tried to avoid jail for a conviction by pretending to be unstable. He figured that a stay in an institution would be easier and shorter than a prison sentence. McMurphy, witty and rebellious, brought meaning to the other patients' lives for a short time. He ended up setting the ward on its ear and stirring up trouble. For his efforts, McMurphy was **lobotomized**. The film, based on Ken Kesey's novel, was a huge success. It won five major Academy Awards in 1975, including Best Picture and Best Actress. Jack Nicholson won his first Oscar for Best Actor for his role in *Cuckoo's Nest*. The book and movie continue to captivate readers and audiences.

Hustlin'

Saturday nights were dance nights. Americans put on their platform shoes and bell-bottomed pants and swarmed the dance clubs. During the sixties, dancers had not needed partners. The seventies brought couples back to the dance floor. Some line dances could be danced alone, but most disco dances required two. Hot singers introduced a series of spins, turns, and steps to be done to their songs. Many disco enthusiasts took dancing seriously. Some rehearsed complicated dance moves during the week before trying them out on the dance floor. The bump, the hustle, and the robot were a few of the many dance crazes of the seventies.

■ Disco competitions were once held across the U.S.

Video Box

In 1975, Sony released its first video cassette recorders (VCRs). They were called Betamax. Later that year, Victor Company of Japan introduced the Video Home System (VHS). It quickly cornered the home entertainment market. No matter which machine Americans chose, the results were similar. People could record television programs and watch them later, often fast-forwarding through the commercials. New businesses sprouted up throughout the country offering pretaped movies and programs for rent. This business boomed as Americans decided to watch movies in the comfort of their own homes. VCRs also gave rise to camcorders, which allowed Americans to video their families and friends and view the tapes on their home systems.

FITNESS FANCY

■ It started with editor James Fixx. He took up running to get in shape and then released his 1978 bestseller *The Complete Book of Running*. Soon, the entire nation was looking at getting into shape. Americans envied the discipline of marathon champion Bill Rogers. Rogers did more than inspire people to be fit. He also marketed a line of athletic clothing. Fitness clothing and equipment became a multi-billion dollar industry in the U.S., and Americans ran right alongside the trendsetters.

Slang

boogie
dance

dig it
know about

far out
awesome; profound

out of sight
excellent, amazing

scene
surroundings or situation

get down
dance

catch my drift
get it; understand

Disco Fever

Americans borrowed many of their fads from the big screen. One of the biggest movies to influence society in the seventies was *Saturday Night Fever*. John Travolta starred as a young man in Brooklyn looking for his place on the dance floor. His style of dancing was disco. The release of the movie in 1978 created a disco craze across the country. Travolta's amazing dance moves and disco fashion inspired inner-city teens to dance, choosing the colored strobe lights and disco clubs over the streets. Dance

clubs, such as Studio 54, became the "in" places to be. Hundreds of people gathered at the club's doors every weekend, hoping that the doorman would choose them to join the party.

By 1980, there were at least 10,000 discos in the U.S., and the industry earned more than $4 billion per year.

■ Stricken with Saturday Night Fever, John Travolta was a disco-dancing machine.

DOWNSIZING

■ Since the Model T of the early 1900s, Americans have loved their automobiles. Many U.S. cars were big and comfortable—the bigger the car, the more successful the driver. With the 1970s energy crisis, big cars became a problem. Incredibly high oil prices, along with long line-ups and limits at the gas pumps, caused many Americans to look for more affordable ways to travel. People began buying smaller cars that would travel farther on a tank of gas. Many of these were foreign-built cars. They were easy to drive, economical, and more environmentally friendly than large cars.

Disco Skating

The disco trend did not stop when night clubs lost popularity. Disco filtered into the streets, where Americans welcomed the newest fad—roller disco. Roller skaters learned disco moves on skates and performed in parks and arenas. Disco music pumped through speakers or earphones, as disco skaters rolled. Many serious roller disco dancers in the late seventies dressed in stretchy,

brightly colored satin pants and entered competitions at roller rinks and in parks. In the mid-seventies, roller skate wheels were being made from a hard plastic called polyurethane. These were quieter than metal or wood wheels, and they allowed skaters to skate faster and more smoothly. Just as *Saturday Night Fever* had started the craze for disco, the movie *Roller Boogie* glorified roller disco.

Burundi Civil War

In 1966, the monarchy in the east-central African country of Burundi was defeated. To take its place, members of the Tutsi tribe established and ran the First Republic. But most people in the country were Hutus, many of whom were poor. They were **oppressed** by the Tutsi elite. The former king, who had been forced out of the country, returned in 1972, hoping to reclaim power. The republic's president, Michel Micombero, quickly quashed the king's efforts. The Hutu wanted change from Tutsi rule and rebelled. The government killed between 100,000 and 150,000 Hutus, wiping out nearly all of the educated Hutus. During the following decades, Hutu-Tutsi clashes claimed hundreds of thousands of lives and nearly destroyed the country.

Lebanese War

In 1970, thousands of Palestinians arrived in Lebanon. Until then, there had been relatively equal numbers of Muslims and Christians in the country. The increase in the Muslim population upset the balance. There had long been conflicts between Muslims and Christians, but on April 13, 1975, an attack at a Christian church sparked a civil war. The attack was followed by retaliation on a busload of Palestinians and other Muslims. In the span of a few weeks, the government had fallen, and bombs were exploding throughout the country. The fighting eased slightly in 1976, but renewed attacks on Israel by a group called the Palestine Liberation Organization (PLO) caused the war to erupt again. The neighboring country of Syria at first helped the Muslims but then withdrew support, fearing Israel would get involved. The fighting was fierce, and the capital city, Beirut, was split in half. Muslims occupied the south, and Christians took the north. In 1978, Israel did invade. Not even 30,000 peacekeepers could stop the fighting. By the end of the decade, around 18,000 Lebanese lives had been lost.

Turkey

Syria

Cyprus

Beirut ●
Lebanon

Mediterranean Sea

Iraq

Israel

Jordan

Saudi Arabia

Gaza Strip

Egypt

N

0   50   100 miles

Religious differences have sparked many conflicts in the Middle East.

■ Many people felt that Pinochet should be tried and punished for his oppressive leadership.

Pinochet's Rule

In 1973, General Augusto Pinochet turned Chile, South America, upside down. The country had been a democracy for around 150 years. Then General Pinochet led a military **coup** against President Salvador Allende. The coup was one of the most violent in South American history—estimates of the number of dead ranged from 5,000 to 30,000. During the coup, President Allende killed himself and Pinochet claimed the presidency. This new leader banned opposition parties in politics and **censored** the media. People who spoke out against the government were often tortured or imprisoned. General Pinochet was harshly criticized for his policies, but his government lowered inflation and encouraged a two-year economic boom in the country. Despite Pinochet's poor human rights record, a vote in 1978 showed that three-quarters of the population supported his rule.

October War

During the Six-Day War in 1967, Israeli forces took over Arab land. This angered the Arabs. On October 5, 1973, when many Israelis were celebrating Yom Kippur, a Jewish holiday, Egypt and Syria attacked Israel. So began what became known as the October War. Syrian troops moved in near the Golan Heights, and Egyptian forces took Sinai. Although Israel was surprised by the attack, it did not take long to mobilize its troops. The U.S. Army provided supplies to help Israel fight its attackers. The Soviet Union assisted the Arab forces. Within a few weeks, Israel had turned back both sides and entered Syria. Then, on October 16, Israeli troops attacked Egypt. The United Nations stepped in and helped stop the fighting by the end of the month. All three parties signed a ceasefire, but relations between them remained strained.

AMIN'S UGANDA

■ In 1971, General Idi Amin took over Uganda, Africa, in a coup. He immediately banned all opposition to his rule. Anyone who acted against him was killed. In 1972, Amin ordered the 60,000 Asians who were not Ugandan citizens to leave the country within ninety days. Many of these people had lived in Uganda for two generations. Some Ugandans resented the Asians because most of them were wealthier than Africans and ran successful businesses. Amin's actions damaged the already weak Ugandan economy. The large tax burden shouldered by the Asian businesspeople was passed on to the overtaxed rural population. As well, production lagged because there were not enough skilled people left in Uganda to replace the Asians who had gone. People around the world condemned the general's actions, but Amin continued with his radical policies. In 1979, forces backed by the African country of Tanzania finally ousted Idi Amin. During his eight years as ruler, as many as 300,000 people were killed by his regime.

Bloody Sunday

On January 30, 1972, demonstrators marched in a civil rights rally in Londonderry, Northern Ireland, to protest British rule. They had done this many times. As before, British soldiers were there to stop them. This time, the soldiers opened fire on the unarmed Irish demonstrators, killing thirteen people. The army insisted that the soldiers fired only after being fired upon. Witnesses disagreed, saying that the protesters were armed with nothing more than rocks. This incident launched a violent revenge spree. On February 2, radicals burned down the British embassy in Dublin. Hostility grew and violence spread. Conflict in the area continued throughout the century.

■ Irish Republican demonstrators were no match for the British military on Bloody Sunday.

"I saw a number of people being shot at the barricade just in front of Rossville Street. It was a terrible situation to be in."

Donncha MacNiallais, an Irish Republican activist

DIGGING DEEP IN CHINA

■ While digging wells In 1975, farmers in northwest Shanxi, a province in China, discovered the tomb of Emperor Shih Huang-ti. Huang-ti had ruled China from from 221 to 206 BCE. An archaeological dig was arranged, and scientists began to excavate the site. What they found in the burial chambers was even more astounding than what had been found in King Tut's tomb in Egypt. The archeologists unearthed around 8,000 life-size ceramic warrior statues, armed with real bows and arrows, spears, and swords. There were also 10,000 pieces of gold, jade, iron, and silk.

Famine in Africa

Drought and famine were nothing new to the people of Ethiopia, a country in northeast Africa. But the early seventies brought with them high prices and no rain for crops. People

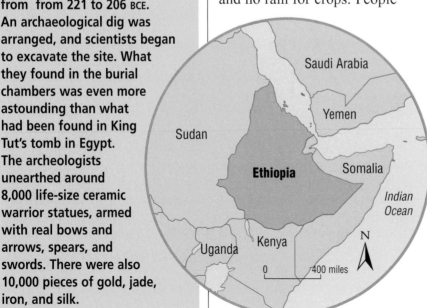

became desperate. Many ate the seed grain that they had hoped to plant for crops. The Ethiopian government did not help the millions of people who were poor and hungry. Money was spent to support military conflicts and to buy weapons instead of food. In only two years, about 1.5 million Ethiopians starved to death.

The government would not allow the media to report on any problems. But a group of university professors visited the area and reported the story of the Ethiopians' struggle to survive. This international attention encouraged other countries to donate food and supplies to the area. Still, many of the donations were misused by the government.

■ Millions of Ethiopians starved as their government waged war.

"The Disappeared"

The 1970s and early 1980s were a time of economic trouble and violence in the South American country of Argentina. A coup, led by Lieutenant General Jorge Rafael Videla, resulted in a military government that ran a reign of terror. People were secretly kidnapped off the streets or from their homes. Most were never seen again. Others citizens were tortured, murdered, or arrested and jailed without a trial, just because they did not support the military government. By 1981, the Argentine Commission for Human Rights in Geneva blamed Videla and his military for 2,300 political murders, 10,000 political arrests, and between 20,000 and 30,000 disappearances.

A group called the Mothers of the Plaza de Mayo began marching each week. They demanded that the government tell them what had happened to their missing sons, daughters, and husbands. The number of people marching for "the disappeared" grew to tens of thousands. International concern for what was happening in Argentina drew celebrities, including recording artist Sting, to the marches.

In 1983, Jorge Videla was arrested and convicted for his crimes. Sentenced to life in prison, he served only five years before being pardoned.

Peace in the Middle East

Egypt and Israel had often shared bullets and harsh words. But they had never shared a visit. That changed in 1977, when Egyptian President Anwar al-Sadat journeyed to Jerusalem. He toured some of the area's most sacred shrines and spoke of peace. While Egypt and Israel were technically at war, al-Sadat and Israeli Prime Minister Menachem Begin shook hands and discussed ways to stop the fighting. A month later, Begin visited Egypt to discuss peace further. U.S. President Jimmy Carter later helped bring an end to the war. Begin and al-Sadat jointly won the Nobel Peace Prize in 1978.

"I come to you today on solid ground to shape a new life and to establish peace."

Anwar al-Sadat

Anwar al-Sadat, Jimmy Carter, and Menachem Begin prepare to sign the peace treaty that will end more than thirty years of war.

Nixon Back in Office

Richard Nixon prepared to settle into his second term as president of the U.S. after winning the November 1972 election. He enjoyed the highest percentage of the vote ever received by a Republican—he won support from 60.7 percent of the voters. After a slim victory four years earlier, Nixon had now won in every state in the country except Massachusetts. He looked forward to achieving peace throughout the world in his remaining four years in office. During Nixon's campaign, an arrest at the Watergate building went virtually unnoticed. The future scandal would spoil Nixon's incredible victory and turn the country against him.

Nixon takes the oath of office to become president.

Cambodia

In 1969, President Nixon began bombing the southeast Asian country of Cambodia. The attacks aimed to wipe out North Vietnamese bases set up along the border. In what was coded as Operation Menu, around 100,000 Cambodians died and another 2 million were left homeless. Then in April 1970, President Nixon sent 40,000 U.S. troops into the area. He said it was not an invasion—it was a necessity. Nixon wanted to protect U.S. units that were withdrawing from Vietnam. Demonstrations sprouted across the country, and many universities and colleges were shut down as a result. Despite this opposition, Nixon continued with the air strikes until 1973.

Watergate Scandal

In 1972, a hotel security guard accidentally discovered an enormous White House scandal. He reported a burglary in progress at Washington's Watergate apartment and office building. The Democratic Party had its headquarters at the Watergate. Police arrested five men who were carrying **eavesdropping** equipment. Two other men, ex-CIA agent E. Howard Hunt and ex-FBI agent G. Gordon Liddy, were arrested shortly afterward. It was quickly discovered that Liddy, Hunt, and burglar James McCord were associated with the campaign to re-elect Republican President Richard Nixon.

The new attorney general launched an investigation. President Nixon had a taping system in his office, so every conversation he had there was recorded. He fought subpoenas ordering him to turn over these tapes to investigators. His own recordings would later prove his knowledge of the burglary and the cover-up.

John Ehrlichman testifies at the Watergate hearings.

SHOT DOWN

George Wallace set his sights high. He had become governor of Alabama and was looking toward the White House. He had campaigned unsuccessfully in 1968, but Wallace was ready to win. In a split second, on May 15, 1972, Arthur Bremer changed Wallace's plans. The 21-year-old Milwaukee man pulled out a gun and shot Governor Wallace in the stomach, arms, shoulder, and spine. Wallace was seriously injured, and doctors feared that he would be permanently paralyzed. He fought back and stayed in the campaign, but he lost the election and never walked again. Bremer was convicted and sentenced to fifty-three years in prison.

> "I'm not a crook."
>
> Richard Nixon

Nixon Resigns

Throughout the course of the Watergate investigation, other illegal activities were linked to the White House. These included illegal campaign contributions and the burglary of a psychiatrist's office to obtain damaging information. In 1974, official impeachment proceedings were set in motion against President Nixon for misusing his power, obstructing justice, and refusing a **subpoena**. Many Americans thought he should be impeached over the Watergate scandal. Instead, on August 9, 1974, he became the first U.S. president to resign. The new president, Gerald Ford, pardoned Nixon a month later. Nixon would never be charged with a crime. While the Watergate scandal stunned Americans, it also showed that the justice system worked. No one, not even the president, was above the law.

Ford Fills Nixon's Shoes

In the wake of the Watergate scandal, people looked to Vice President Gerald Ford for stability. When Nixon resigned as president in 1974, Ford became the thirty-eighth president of the U.S. He had to find a way to rebuild Americans' trust in the government. He hoped that by pardoning Nixon he would heal the nation's wounds. Many Americans felt the former president should face criminal charges and that a pardon should not have been granted until Nixon publicly admitted what he had done. Ford pushed on and tried to improve the country's struggling economy, which he called "Public Enemy No. 1." As Ford's term came to a close, he promised to continue the policies that he thought would bring an end to the economic trouble in the country. He went head-to-head with Jimmy Carter and lost the presidency in a close race in 1976.

Twice Lucky

Gerald Ford was in office for four years. In that time, two women shot at him on two separate occasions. First, a member of the **Manson family**, Lynette "Squeaky" Fromme, pulled out a gun and pointed it at the president in Sacramento, California, on September 5, 1975. The gun jammed and would not fire. She was quickly arrested. Seventeen days later in San Francisco, Sara Jane Moore pulled a gun and fired it once at the president. A bystander saw what she was doing and knocked her arm, so she missed her target. The stray bullet hit a planter close to the president, bounced off the sidewalk, and then hit a cab driver. Both women were sentenced to life in prison for their assassination attempts.

■ Lynette Fromme is handcuffed and detained by Secret Service agents after pointing a gun at the president.

Pentagon Papers

Daniel Ellsberg, a government consultant, helped put together a history of U.S. policy in Vietnam. When Richard Nixon became president, people did not want to read about it, but Ellsberg and others wanted the public to know the truth. In 1971, the *New York Times* and the *Washington Post* published bits and pieces of this top-secret report about the government's involvement in Vietnam. What was dubbed the "Pentagon Papers" studied policies dating back to Harry Truman's presidency in the 1940s and 1950s. The report created a great deal of controversy. The pages detailed lies and mistakes made by government and military leaders. The study alleged that President Johnson had sent troops to Vietnam, while at the same time telling Americans that he did not plan to engage in war. It also stated that the Vietnam War was fought more to avoid

■ Daniel Ellsberg's report exposed the truth about U.S. involvement in Vietnam.

a humiliating U.S. defeat than to help the South Vietnamese.

The government charged Ellsberg with violating secrecy laws, but the charges were dropped in 1973. He became a hero to peace activists, and many more people began to call for an end to the war in Vietnam.

PANAMA CANAL

■ The Panama Canal was in the headlines in 1977. Control of the waterway was under question because no Panamanian had signed the 1903 treaty that gave the U.S. power over the canal. Panamanians resented American control, and President Jimmy Carter wanted to set things right. He was the fourth president in a row to tackle this issue. Carter made an unpopular decision: he gave control of the canal to Panama. This meant that Panama would gradually take over the canal as well as the 533-square-mile strip of land surrounding it. The U.S., however, would still have the right to defend the area.

Many of the 10,000 Americans living on this land disliked Carter's agreement. So did a large number of people in the U.S. Despite this, Carter was determined that the U.S. should act fairly in its dealings with other countries. A future president disagreed. In the 1980s, President George Bush used force in Panama against President Manuel Noriega. Noriega was taken to the U.S., and jailed for drug offenses.

Carter's America

In 1976, U.S. voters were on the edge of their seats during the federal election. When all the ballots were counted, Democrat Jimmy Carter had won the presidency of the U.S. in one of the closest races of the century. It was not an easy time to govern the country. As promised, Carter pardoned draft-dodgers who had left the country during the Vietnam War. This was a very controversial action. Also, high unemployment and inflation threatened U.S. economic strength. Throughout his term, Carter tried to bring down inflation by asking businesses to keep prices low. He appealed to labor leaders to discourage their workers from demanding huge pay raises. He cut spending and added taxes on imported oil to help offset the problems.

Other countries were also causing problems for the U.S. U.S. and Soviet relations had reached an all-time low. At the same time, President Carter was trying to free U.S. hostages being held in Tehran. Carter moved forward in spite of the obstacles. He was a player in bringing China and the U.S. closer together. He also helped to arrange the peace treaty between Israel and Egypt. These achievements were not enough. In 1980, Carter lost the election to the California governor, Ronald Reagan.

Call Her Ms.

In the spring of 1972, *Ms.* was launched. This new magazine was geared toward a growing sector of the population: **feminists**. Gloria Steinem created the publication with the help of an all-female staff. The staff aimed to help women take control of their lives by presenting articles about strong women written by strong women. *Ms.* sold all 300,000 copies of the first issue in slightly more than a week. Warner Communications invested $1 million in the magazine, ensuring its financial security. The success of *Ms.* proved to

■ Gloria Steinem and Patricia Carbine were key players in the growing women's rights movement.

some skeptics that feminism was here to stay and that the movement was strong enough to warrant an ongoing magazine.

Autobiography Bust

In 1972, the literary world eagerly awaited *The Autobiography of Howard Hughes*. The book's author was Clifford Irving, a novelist. McGraw-Hill publishers paid Irving $765,000 for a book about Hughes, a billionaire **recluse**. Irving claimed he wrote the book with Hughes after more than 100 interviews with the famous industrialist.

Two weeks before the book was to be published, Irving stopped the presses. He confessed that he had not talked to Hughes at all. The book was complete fiction, right down to the anecdotes and the notes that were believed to be in Hughes' own handwriting. Irving pleaded guilty to charges of fraud on March 16, 1972, and he and his wife served seventeen months in prison for the hoax. In 2000, the most famous book that

> "I wrote the autobiography of the life Howard Hughes would have lived if he dared."
>
> Clifford Irving

was never published was finally made available to the public through Terrificbooks, which Irving co-owned. It was sold only over the Internet.

Sophie's Choice

William Styron's 1979 novel, *Sophie's Choice*, took a look at the ugly side of humanity. It was the story of a young writer named Stingo and the neighbor he grew to love—Sophie. Sophie was a Polish woman who had survived the Holocaust of World War II. After the war, she lived with an abusive man and turned to Stingo for support. As the story twists and turns, the reader is invited to share the horror that Sophie experienced at the hands of the Nazis. She was made to choose between her two children—one would be killed and the other would be sent to a youth camp with a chance of surviving. The choice Sophie makes haunts her and eventually leads to her death. The powerful novel was made into a popular movie in 1982. Meryl Streep won an Academy Award for her role as Sophie in the film.

■ Among William Styron's awards are a Pulitzer Prize and a National Medal of Arts.

The World According to Irving

John Irving was an English teacher at Mount Holyoke College in South Hadley, Massachusetts. In 1969, his first novel, *Setting Free the Bears*, was published. He wrote two more over the next five years. Then, in 1978, Irving caught the attention of U.S. readers with *The World According to Garp*. This story followed the ups and downs in the marriage and life of a writer. It was an enormous success. Irving was nominated for the National Book Award and the National Book Critics Circle Award. *Garp* allowed Irving to leave his teaching job and write full time. His other popular novels include *The Cider House Rules* (1985), *A Prayer for Owen Meany* (1989) and *A Widow for One Year* (1998).

War and Remembrance

Many of Herman Wouk's books were drawn from his experiences fighting in World War II. His third novel, written in 1951, was *The Caine Mutiny*. The novel told the story of Navy sailors and the bizarre behavior of their captain. It earned Wouk the Pulitzer Prize for fiction and was made into a Broadway play.

Wouk, the son of Jewish immigrants from Russia, was born in New York City. After obtaining a degree from Columbia University, Wouk began his career as a comedy writer for a radio station in 1935. Then the war broke out, and Wouk **enlisted** in the army. While overseas, he began to work on his first novel. He wrote five novels between 1947 and 1962. In the 1970s, Wouk published

two bestsellers. *The Winds of War* (1971) was a romance novel. It told of events in the first years of World War II, from just before the beginning of the war to the bombing at Pearl Harbor. Its sequel, *War and Remembrance* (1978), told the story of a Jewish woman who was sent to a concentration camp. The books were so popular that they were turned into television miniseries.

Unlucky Thirteen

It was supposed to be simple—the third landing on the moon. But in April 1970, the spacecraft *Apollo 13* drew millions of Americans to their televisions to see if the astronauts would make it home.

As *Apollo 13* was nearing the moon, one of the oxygen tanks had blown up and disabled the other. Astronauts relied on these tanks for breathing

■ Nobody expected that the *Apollo 13* mission would come as close as it did to fatal failure.

and to fuel the electrical systems. Without these reserves, the astronauts would likely not have enough oxygen to return to Earth. The crew transferred into the lunar module, *Aquarius*, which was meant just for landing on the moon. It was not equipped to support three people. The crew then shut down their main command module to save energy until they needed to re-enter Earth's atmosphere. The lunar module had its own power

and oxygen, and the astronauts used as little power as possible during their three-day return to Earth. They overcame near-freezing temperatures and too much carbon dioxide in the lunar module, and they landed safely in the Pacific Ocean on April 17. The entire country breathed a sigh of relief as the crew emerged from the module.

> "Okay, Houston, we've had a problem"
>
> John L. Swigert, Jr. *Apollo 13* astronaut

TOWERING ABOVE

■ In 1973, Americans were at the top. The Sears Tower in Chicago was completed, becoming the tallest building in the world. The 110-story building was 1,454 feet high and spread across two city blocks. It held 4.5 million square feet of office space, and used about as much power as a town of 35,000 people. The amazing Sears Tower was designed by the architectural firm Skidmore, Owings, and Merrill. It was built by Sears, Roebuck, and Company in less than two-and-a-half years. On a clear day, four states are visible from the observation deck on the 103rd floor—Illinois, Indiana, Michigan, and Wisconsin. Before this structure was built, the Empire State Building in New York had held the title of tallest building.

Ingenious Discovery

Led by Dr. Har Gobind Khorana, a team of scientists at the Massachusetts Institute of Technology made history in 1976. They created the first man-made **gene** that could work inside a cell. Unlike previous genes, this one was completely manufactured— a natural gene was not used as a model. The biochemists had put together a gene that corrects **mutations**. This discovery was met with mixed feelings. Such a discovery could, down the road, help prevent hereditary diseases. It could also be used in **genetic engineering**. This made some Americans very nervous. The debate over genetic engineering carried through into the twenty-first century.

An Apple a Day

Stephen Wozniak and Steven Jobs designed a computer circuit board in Jobs' California garage in 1976. The Apple I was sold without a monitor, keyboard, or casing. The following year, the company introduced the personal computer, Apple II, and it released another model, Apple III, in 1980. The Apple III did not sell well because it was very expensive and had hardware problems. Apple worked out the bugs in the system, and by 1982, it became the first personal-computer company to achieve annual sales of $1 billion. Apple continues to develop and market new personal computers.

■ The Apple computer changed technology forever.

Being Green

Concern about the health of the environment led to the first officially recognized Earth Day on April 22, 1970. This first Earth awareness day included seminars, parades, and recycling fairs. The federal government also realized the importance of protecting the environment. In 1972, the Environmental Protection Agency was established. The United Nations assisted in raising awareness by holding an environmental conference in Sweden. This was not enough for some activists. Many people joined environmental groups and demanded a change in policies from companies that were polluting the environment. Green fever hit Americans hard, and more people insisted that resources be used responsibly. Activists argued that humans had a duty to manage the natural environment responsibly. Through their efforts, many international environmental policies have been developed.

■ People around the world rallied behind the environmental cause on the first Earth Day in 1970.

SUPERSONIC

■ In 1977, the world's first supersonic passenger plane took off from Kennedy Airport in New York. It held 100 passengers and flew twice as fast as other airplanes. After nearly ten years of technical glitches and financial problems, the Concorde was at last in the air. It had been a long, hard-won battle for the French and British builders. The Concorde was surrounded by controversy. Many people warned of environmental damage to Earth's atmosphere if such planes were permitted to fly. Others fought against the deafening sound the Concorde produced. Despite these concerns, the Concorde passed all requirements and began offering service across the Atlantic Ocean.

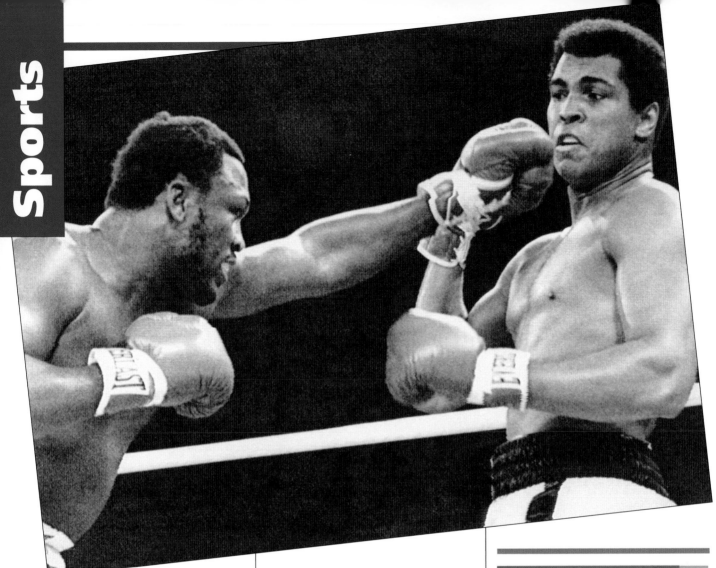

Muhammad Ali dodges Joe Frazier's lunge during the famous "Thrilla in Manila."

Ringside Champions

Joe Frazier was an Olympic boxing champion and a fierce competitor in the ring. In 1971, Frazier was the World Boxing Association (WBA) champion. He was pitted against Muhammad Ali, the World Boxing Council (WBC) champion. Neither man had lost a bout. Frazier won the match by **decision**. Ali waited three years for a chance to fight Frazier again. In 1974, Ali beat Frazier by decision, but it was not the last time the two great boxers would meet.

In 1975, Frazier and Ali faced each other in the Philippines, in a match that would become known as the "Thrilla in Manila." On October 1, around 700 million people in 65 countries watched the fight on television. Ali was incredible. Frazier's trainer threw in the towel to stop the match before the final bell. It was one of the greatest fights in boxing history. Frazier retired in 1976, leaving an impressive career with thirty-two victories, four defeats, and one draw. Ali went on to become one of few heavyweight boxers to win back a world championship title twice—once in 1974 and again in 1978.

OLYMPIC SUCCESS

U.S. swimmer Mark Spitz made history at the 1972 Olympic Games in Munich, Germany. He took the gold medal for the 100-meter and 200-meter freestyle. He also dominated the 100-meter and 200-meter butterfly races. Spitz set world records for each of these individual events. The talented athlete joined other U.S. swimmers in the 400-meter and 800-meter freestyle relay teams. Then he swam the butterfly in the 400-meter medley relay. His relay teams also set world records. At the end of the competition, Spitz had claimed an incredible seven gold medals for the Red, White, and Blue.

RLD FOCUS

PERFECT TEN

The sweetheart of the 1976 Olympic Games in Montreal, Canada, was an 86-pound, 14-year-old Romanian gymnast. Nadia Comaneci redefined the limits of gymnastics as she flipped, twirled, and leaped her way onto the podium. She scored seven perfect 10s, the highest possible score in gymnastics. Comaneci won three gold medals, a silver, and a bronze. The young athlete went on to win several other international competitions, but none was as spectacular as her Olympic showing. Comaneci defected to the U.S. in 1989.

College Hoops

On March 26, 1979, all eyes were on the National College Athletic Association (NCAA) basketball championships. The final was a showdown between Indiana State and Michigan State, but it was not the teams that drew the attention. It was the talented stars who led each side. Indiana's forward, Larry Bird, and Michigan's hero, Earvin "Magic" Johnson, were the best college players in the country. Their amazing moves and awesome talent sent college basketball television ratings through the roof. That night, Johnson came out ahead of Bird in the championship match, but their competition was not over. The two stars carried their rivalry into the professionals, both finding great success in the National Basketball Association (NBA). Bird led the Celtics to victory three times and Johnson dunked the Lakers to the championships five times. Each star was named Most Valuable Player in the league three times. Together, they electrified basketball fans and made it the sport to watch into the 1980s.

Ashe on Fire

In 1975, two U.S. tennis stars competed for the Wimbledon title. The favorite, Jimmy Connors, faced off against the talented Arthur Ashe. Ashe won the match in four sets and became the first African American to win the prestigious tournament. He was also the sport's first African-American millionaire. Ashe won fifty-one professional tournaments, always with grace and dignity. He was forced to retire due to heart disease in 1980, and he died thirteen years later.

■ Ashe's powerful serve helped him to become a tennis legend.

> **"All I could think about was that I wanted to touch all the bases."**
>
> Hank Aaron on his record-breaking home run

■ Hank Aaron was one of baseball's best.

Olympic Massacre

The international camaraderie of the Olympic Games was lost at the 1972 Olympics in Munich, Germany. On September 5, eight Palestinian **guerrillas,** who called themselves Black September, broke into the Olympic Village. They stormed the Israeli athletes' quarters and shot and killed two coaches. In the flurry of bullets, fourteen team members managed to escape, but nine others were taken hostage. Outside, German police officers surrounded the building.

The terrorists wanted the Israeli government to release 200 Palestinians imprisoned in Israel. Israeli Prime Minister Golda Meir refused to give in to the guerrillas. After negotiations, the terrorists agreed to a safe escape to Cairo with the hostages, who would then be freed. At the airport, police snipers opened fire as two of the terrorists approached the airplane. A shoot-out followed. In the end, a German police officer, five terrorists, and all the hostages lay dead. The Olympic Committee decided that the Games should continue. The rest of the Israeli team left Germany to mourn the tragedy.

Hank Aaron Hits it Big

At the age of fifteen, Hank Aaron started playing shortstop for the Mobile Black Bears, a semiprofessional baseball team. The following year, in 1952, Aaron signed with the Milwaukee Braves, which would soon become the Atlanta Braves. He played his first major league game in 1954. Over the next nineteen years, Aaron played well, drawing praise for both his batting and his outfielding. Meanwhile, he was nearing Babe Ruth's career home run record of 714.

Late in 1973, Aaron hit his 713th career home run. But he would have to wait until the next season to try to break the record. He received hate mail from people who resented that an African American was so close to claiming one of baseball's prized records. By the beginning of the 1974 season, Aaron's family had been placed under police protection. Aaron did not back down. His first swing of the season gave him the home run that tied Babe Ruth's record. Four days later, he hit his 715th home run at his home diamond. Hammerin' Hank had claimed the home run record. At the time of Aaron's retirement in 1976, he held several career records, including most home runs (755), most runs batted in (2,297), and most extra-base hits (1,477). He was inducted into the Baseball Hall of Fame in 1982.

Billy Jean on Top

In the early 1970s, Billie Jean King proved that she was the best female tennis player in America. She was the first woman to win more than $100,000 in competition. She paved the way for other female athletes, and she fought for equality with men's tennis. King won four U.S. Open singles titles, and she basked in a 1973 victory against Bobby Riggs. She accused him of being a male chauvinist, and she promised to teach him what a woman could do. In front of more than 30,000 stadium fans and millions more glued to their television sets, King beat the arrogant ex-champ Riggs on the court. King inspired the women's movement and fought to establish a separate tennis tour for women.

Billy Jean King was a success on and off the court. She was strong advocate of the women's movement and a crusader for gay and lesbian rights.

Undefeated Dolphins

A few professional football teams have come close to having undefeated seasons, but in 1972, the Miami Dolphins actually did it. They became the first National Football League team to finish an entire season without losing or tying a single game. With talent such as Paul Warfield, Bob Griese, Larry Csonka, and Mercury Morris, the Dolphins finished the regular season with fourteen wins, no losses. Then they won the next two division playoff games. They made it to the Super Bowl, beating the favored Washington Redskins 14-7. The Dolphins took home the title and made sporting history.

"If another team is good enough to go undefeated, more power to them. We will always be the first to have done that, which nobody can take away."

Miami Dolphin Bob Griese

Conflict Over Color

The issues of race relations have plagued the U.S. for decades. For years, African-American students could not attend certain schools. Many civil rights groups objected to this policy and lobbied to have African-American children fully **integrated** into all schools. In the 1970s, the **segregation** policy was questioned. Despite resistance from some Americans, in 1974 many cities were ordered to continue busing students to other schools so that all children, regardless of race, would study together. Nearly half of all students were bused into other neighborhoods. Riots over the court order followed. Some Americans boycotted the participating schools and would not allow their children to attend classes with African-American students. Many African-American students were attacked as they tried to enter their schools. Some schools allowed only the minimum number of African-American students that the ruling demanded. Civil rights groups continued to fight for equality throughout the decade.

> "They are taught to hate us. How can you learn anything if you're afraid of being stabbed?"
>
> A student on forced busing

■ Everything looks as jumbled as the above headline for people who cannot read. In 1976, studies showed that around 15 percent of U.S. adults could not functionally read or write. To be functionally illiterate means that a person cannot read or write well enough to meet the demands of day-to-day life. The study showed that an alarming number of people could not interpret instructions on labels, read to their children, or decipher street signs. In light of this shocking statistic, many organizations began pushing for help from the government to teach people to read.

Women's Rights

Women's rights were a serious issue in the 1970s. Women fought for equality across the country. On August 26, 1970, thousands of women marched in New York—police estimated the crowd at 10,000, while demonstrators insisted that there were upwards of 50,000. Women demanded that they be paid the same as men for similar work. At the time, women received on average only 58.2 percent of what a man was paid for the same job. Marches were also held in New Orleans, San Francisco, Detroit, Indianapolis, and Los Angeles.

Then 1975 was declared International Women's Year. Feminist issues were discussed, and seminars were offered to help women gain control of their lives and futures. Meetings were open to both men and women. The lectures aimed to change attitudes about women, and they made people rethink traditional

■ Women's rights activists protest for control over their own bodies.

roles. Why should young girls be placed in home economics classes and young boys in shop? Why are men considered the workers? The conferences also aimed to get government to pass laws that would make things equal for women. Notable women, including Gloria Steinem, became involved in the conferences and encouraged women to speak up. The feminist movement continued to gain momentum throughout the seventies and eighties.

Radicalism

The 1970s were turbulent years when angry young students created underground organizations to fight for their causes. Many of these groups used violence to promote peace. In 1970, four students blew up a campus laboratory to protest the university's involvement in war research. The blast killed one graduate student and did $1.5 million in damages. A few months later, two university students against the Vietnam War decided to overthrow the capitalist system by robbing a bank. A police officer was killed during this crime. The robbers went into hiding, and one, Katherine Ann Power, finally gave herself up in 1993. She was the longest-running radical outlaw on the Most Wanted List. Other people, including the Catholic priest Father Daniel Berrigan, were convicted for burning draft records and encouraging riots at demonstrations.

■ Throughout the seventies, protests were commonplace. Americans embraced the right to assemble in groups.

The New Family

Before the 1970s, couples who were unable to have children or adopt could not have a family. A British couple changed the traditional family forever. Gilbert and Lesley Brown invested $1,500 into the experiment of two doctors. After eighty tries, the doctors became the first to create a "test-tube baby." While this phrase did not represent what really happened with the "in-vitro" procedure, it attracted the attention of the world. The egg was fertilized in a laboratory, but it was carried by the woman, who gave birth to a baby girl on July 25, 1975.

A couple in New York sued their doctor for destroying their egg in 1972. The doctors at the hospital had thought the procedure was too risky. The couple claimed that the doctors played God when they killed a potential life. They were awarded $50,000. The in-vitro procedure gave rise to debate around the world. Some people thought that science should not interfere with nature. Others feared that this procedure would lead to engineered babies. Supporters argued that if science could give a couple a baby, no one was justified in denying them.

BICENTENNIAL BASH

■ In 1976, Americans joined in the celebration of the nation's 200th birthday. The party officially started on July 4, when the sun rose over Maine, which is the country's northeasternmost location. Large and small cities alike hosted festivities for the country's birthday. New York City put on Operation Sail, a regatta of ships in the harbor. The residents of George, Washington, baked a 60-square-foot cherry pie to honor its namesake. The birthday bash helped to unite Americans.

During the oil crisis, Americans were forced to wait in long lines or even make appointments to buy gasoline.

In 1971, President Nixon was fighting inflation with both barrels. For three months, he froze wages and prices. This meant that salary and price increases were not allowed. After the three-month period, the freeze began to thaw slightly. Nixon introduced a one-year time frame during which wages and prices could rise again, but not by very much. Prices were allowed to go up only enough to cover costs but not to increase profits. Workers were not allowed raises in pay that covered past work. Wages could increase by no more than 6.6 percent each year. Nixon continued to fight inflation until his resignation in 1974.

Oil Crisis

In the 1970s, people discovered the economic impact of oil. Those who had oil had power. Those who did not, needed it. The U.S. claimed only around 6 percent of the world's population, but it used one-third of the energy resources. This became a problem in 1973. The Organization of Petroleum Exporting Countries (OPEC) raised the price of oil by nearly 200 percent within a few months. It put a similar **embargo** in place against any other country that supported Israel. OPEC members included Iran, Kuwait, Saudi Arabia, and Qatar. Much of the world experienced an energy crisis. In an effort to conserve energy, President Nixon tried to reduce the speed limit to 50 miles per hour. The embargo was lifted in 1974 after the U.S. helped establish a ceasefire in the October War. The crisis showed the world that the new economic powers were countries with oil wells.

"In view of the increase in support for Israel, the Saudi Arabian Kingdom has decided to stop the export of oil to the United States of America for adopting such a stand."

A press release from the Saudi Arabian government

Tough Times

In 1976, the U.S. unemployment rate went through the roof. It rose for three months in a row, and an estimated 25.9 million U.S. people were living in poverty. This was the largest number since 1970. Then, in 1979, inflation hit a high all over the world. People made less money but continued to spend. As a result, more money circulated and the inflation rate rose. The inflation rate reached 172 percent in Argentina, and the rate hit double digits in France and Britain. It neared 15 percent in the U.S. The skyrocketing prices for oil and gas as a result of the OPEC crisis added fuel to the fire. For Americans, the seventies ended with a nervous eye toward the economy.

Alaskan Black Gold

After three years of construction, the enormous pipeline was at last finished. In June 1977, oil began flowing through the Alaska pipeline to the rest of the country. The lines ran from Prudhoe Bay's North Slope oil fields to refineries in Valdez on Prince William Sound. This Alaskan oil reserve was one of North America's richest supplies. More than $9 billion had been spent setting up the pipelines. They were built to pump 2 million barrels of petroleum out of the oilfield each day. The more than 800 miles of pipe crossed 800 rivers. The first oil piped through the pipeline reached refineries on July 28. The oil drawn from this field allowed the U.S. to reduce imports from the Middle East and other oil-rich regions by 15 percent.

New York City Loan

In 1975, New York City was on the verge of bankruptcy, and people were looking to the federal government for help. President Ford announced that he would block Congress's attempt to arrange a loan. The next day, a *New York Times* headline read "Ford to City: Drop Dead." The pressure that resulted caused Ford to change his mind. Many people feared that a financial collapse in New York City would cause serious problems in worldwide banking. Ford finally agreed to help the New York City government stay afloat. The huge city was about to **default** on loans, so President Ford signed legislation permitting the Federal Treasury to lend $2.3 billion to the city each year for three years. This bailout was aimed at helping New York cover its monthly debt payments of nearly $1 billion. Ford insisted that part of the loan be paid back every year. Some taxpayers argued that the government should not have stepped in. They thought it was a drain on tax money.

▬ Before President Ford approved the New York City loan, citizens were hit with large tax increases. Many municipal services were cut, and thousands of jobs were lost.

ECONOMIC TURBULENCE

▬ In the 1970s, the U.S. faced several economic challenges. The trade deficit soared, while gold reserves shrank. Inflation and unemployment rates skyrocketed. To try to prevent a serious problem, President Nixon stopped gold payments in 1971. Unbacked by gold, the U.S. dollar had to re-establish itself against other currencies in the world. Many other countries that put their money up against the U.S. dollar could no longer do so. No country's money had a fixed value compared to another. The dollar fell in comparison to the Japanese yen and West German mark. In December 1971, ten of the world's leading non-communist countries met to end the money crisis. After the meeting of the Group of Ten, a system of controlled rates was introduced into international commerce policy.

Imitating Hair Styles

In 1976, Olympic gold-medalist Dorothy Hamill captivated Americans. Her flawless jumps and spins on the blades of her figure skates brought her international attention. But her haircut brought her fame. Many people tried to imitate the "Hamill wedge." All over the country, women cropped their hair in a bob, just like Dorothy's.

Not all women favored the figure skater's hairstyle. Some preferred the Farrah Fawcett look. Fawcett's big, blonde, feathered hair drove women

■ Dorothy Hamill's geometrically angled bob started a trend in women's hairstyles.

to their hairstylists by the thousands, all trying to capture the breathtaking look of their favorite Charlie's Angel. Farrah Fawcett dolls, posters, and advertisements gave women

the chance to study Fawcett's style—and try to copy it. The Hollywood superstar affected fashion sensibility all across the nation.

Saying No to the Midi

In 1970, the calf-length midi dress promised to be "the" style of the year. U.S. women did not agree. They preferred the shorter mini skirts they had grown used to throughout the sixties. Other women were comfortable in jeans or pants. They did not want to buy a new wardrobe every time designers released new styles. To show their feelings, many women kept on dressing the way they had been doing, and they left midi dresses hanging on store racks.

Funky Footwear

What Americans wore on their feet said a great deal about them. Footwear in the seventies was a definite fashion statement—"I have style." Thick-soled, open-backed shoes called clogs became a hit with both men and women. For those riding the fitness wave, sneakers were the footwear of choice. Sandals

and platform shoes became must-haves for fashion-conscious Americans. Some women leaned toward high boots that laced up to the knees. The boots were most often worn with hot pants, which were short shorts. This look had also been popular in the sixties and was carried into the early seventies by disco stars and Hollywood actors.

Seventies Fads

To be truly fashionable in the seventies meant being "hip." Cruising in the car, dressed in the coolest bell-bottoms and platform shoes, was not enough. The seventies fashion plate needed tunes. Eight-track cassettes featuring the best disco hits littered the dashboards of nearly every car. Portable tape players were designed so that people could take their music with them. Walking down the street with a transistor radio was a sign of coolness. By the mid-seventies, the eight-track fad was replaced by cassettes.

■ Eight-track tapes were one of the first portable music mediums.

Disco Style

The late seventies were ruled by disco. To stay hip, Americans had to know how to dress. For many, their model was John Travolta, the disco king. He inspired U.S. men to don flashy suits with silky shirts opened to mid-chest to show off the gold chains around their necks. The suit pants had to be bell-bottoms. Disco dancing was best done in a pair of clunky platform shoes.

Women's disco-dancing style came from celebrities, too. Many dancers borrowed the look of the Swedish singing sensation ABBA. Women painted powder-

■ ABBA was one of the most successful disco groups of all time.

blue eye shadow (or shadow fashioned in a rainbow) on their lids. Some added a string of tiny rhinestones to their eyelids for extra glitz. They also copied ABBA's skin-tight satin pants, matching satin shirts, and high-heeled shoes. Some women preferred off-the-shoulder, loose dresses to dance in. Regardless of the style, many Americans waited eagerly for the weekend, when they could dress up and dance the night away.

CASUAL CLOTHING

■ The 1970s was an era of easy-going styles. Fashion came from the streets, not from a designer's new line of clothing. Americans wore what was comfortable. High school and college students loved blue jeans and T-shirts. Sleeveless tops and muscle shirts also gained popularity with both men and women. Women embraced the new hip-hugging clothing that showed off their curves. They had fought for equality and expressed this by wearing pants, not dresses, to work and out on the town. Velvet or satin pant suits turned heads in the seventies.

Draft-dodging Emigrants

In the late 1960s and 1970s, thousands of young U.S. men escaped the draft by moving to Canada. These young men were opposed to the Vietnam War and did not want to enlist.

In Canada, people could enter the country and then apply for landed immigrant status. After the Vietnam War ended, this easy-going policy began to disappear. By 1980, draft-dodgers, who were criticized at home, were no longer allowed to apply for citizenship from within Canada.

QUOTAS ALTERED

An amendment to the Immigration and Nationality Act in 1978 made some changes to the country's quotas—the number of immigrants allowed into the country each year. The amendment got rid of separate quotas for each of the world's hemispheres and introduced an annual global quota of 290,000, with a maximum of 20,000 from any one country. But more than the official maximum were often admitted to the U.S. Between 1976 and 1985, immigration ranged from a 1977 total of 398,089 (4,701 of whom were refugees) to the 1980 total of 796,356 (201,552 of whom were refugees). The average yearly number of immigrants in that ten-year period sat at about 546,000, which was 88 percent higher than the official quota.

Vietnamese people packed into a boat making its way to Hong Kong.

The Plight of the Boat People

The Vietnam War was over, but fighting continued in Southeast Asia. By 1977, thousands of people were fleeing Cambodia, Laos, and South Vietnam every month. By the end of the year, around 5.6 million of these people had left their homes. Faced with violence and **persecution** in their home countries, the refugees loaded into boats and took their chances on the ocean. Many people died on the way. Others ended up in Asian countries that could no longer handle the number of new people. Hong Kong, the Philippines, Indonesia, and Malaysia stopped accepting refugees. The U.S. accepted 165,000 "boat people" in the two years following Communism's victory over Democracy in Asia. In 1977, the U.S. government set a limit of 15,000 each year. That number was raised to 25,000 in 1978 and then to 50,000 in 1979. The flow of Southeast Asian immigrants continued through the 1990s and into the 2000s.

LEGAL AND ILLEGAL IMMIGRATION

■ The recorded number of immigrants in a nation is rarely the actual number of people who came into the country. Illegal immigrants enter without following immigration procedures. In 1977, the Illegal Alien Task Force was established to look into the amount of illegal immigration. The committee reported that there were between 6 and 8 million illegal aliens in the U.S. In 1976, about 876,000 illegal aliens were caught, compared to only 89,000 in 1961.

Of the immigrants who gained citizenship through the proper channels in the 1970s, most were from Asian and Latin-American countries.

Immigrants Admitted as Refugees		
1972–1973	Ugandan Asians	1,500
1973–1979	Soviets	35,758
1975–1979	Chileans	1,400
1976–1977	Chileans, Bolivians, Uruguayans	343
1978–1979	Lebanese	1,000
1979	Cuban prisoners	15,000

LEGAL IMMIGRATION BETWEEN 1970–1979

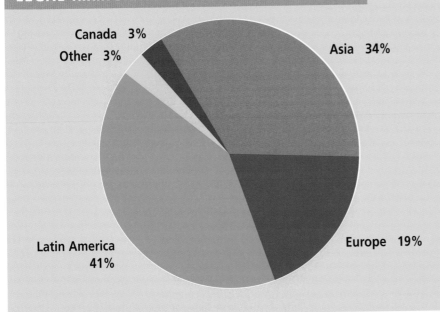

Canada 3%
Other 3%
Asia 34%
Europe 19%
Latin America 41%

Brain Drain

At the end of September 1977, U.S. immigration policies drew international attention. Among the 189,378 men and women given U.S. citizenship in the previous year, 24 percent of the total and 40 percent of the Asian and African immigrants were trained, skilled individuals. The U.S. was accused of practicing favoritism, attracting professional and technical people. Other countries, especially less-developed ones, charged that the U.S. was taking part in a "brain drain." These governments argued that they could not compete with what the U.S. offered to skilled individuals. The United Nations estimated that the U.S. regained around 11 percent of the economic and technical assistance that Washington had sent to less-developed countries by granting citizenship to talented people who were not America-trained. The U.S. was not the worst offender, though: Switzerland took 24 percent, Sweden took 31 percent, West Germany claimed 40 percent, and Austria regained 72 percent. Percentages aside, the U.S. attracted more skilled workers than any other country.

Non-Quota Immigrants

Sometimes the U.S. allowed people to enter the country even though the quota had been reached. Many times, these people claimed refugee status. This meant that their lives would be in danger or they would be persecuted if they returned to their home country. Throughout the 1970s, civil unrest and war created a large number of refugees. Refugees made up approximately 10 percent of the total immigration to the U.S. during the 1970s.

Macho Men

Many people thought the disco group the Village People would have one hit and then fade away. The band surprised everyone, including themselves. The Village People's first song, "Macho Man," reached number twenty-five on the charts in 1978. This hit performance featured the group dressed as a police officer, a cowboy, a construction worker, a Native American, an athlete, and a leatherman. The album sold an astounding 1 million copies. The Village People were named 1978's disco group of the year at Billboard's International Disco Forum, beating out the Bee Gees for the honor.

In 1978, the Village People released *Cruisin'*, which contained their smash hit, "YMCA." It reached number two on the Billboard charts and sold 2 million copies. The following year, the group released *Go West* and the single "In the Navy," which hit number three. The band was lighthearted and funny, which had been their purpose from the start. They stayed on top for three years before becoming history with the seventies.

■ The Village People will always be remembered for their interesting costumes and catchy tunes.

FLYING HIGH

■ The Eagles soared in the 1970s. The band released its self-titled album in 1972, which boasted two number-one hits— "Take it Easy" and "Witchy Woman." The group's 1975 album, *One of These Nights*, produced number-one hits in the title song and "Best of My Love." The same year, The Eagles won their first Grammy Award for "Lyin' Eyes." Then *Eagles: Their Greatest Hits 1971–1975* became one of the best-selling records in rock music history.

The band took off in 1976, with the album *Hotel California*. The title track made The Eagles a household name and won a Grammy Award in 1977. Two years later, the band released its last album of original songs, *The Long Run*. The musicians then set out to launch successful solo careers. In 1994, The Eagles reunited for a tour and released their fourth number-one album, *Hell Freezes Over*. They were inducted into the Rock and Roll Hall of Fame in 1998.

The King Is Dead

No one could believe it. The King of Rock and Roll was dead. Elvis Presley died from a heart attack in 1977 at his Graceland mansion in Memphis, Tennessee. He was 42 years old. Presley had become a legend, with his swiveling hips and unique brand of blues music. The star had connected with a generation that needed something to call their own, something a little rebellious that their parents did not approve of. His hit songs "Love Me Tender," "Jailhouse Rock," and "Don't Be Cruel," along with such movies as *Viva Las Vegas*, kept women swooning and men trying to be just like him. Elvis Presley had an enormous following around the world, and his death struck fans hard.

People rushed to Memphis with flowers and comforting words for other mourners. Fans held all-night **vigils**. Some even insisted that the King was still alive. They were convinced that he had faked his own death. Fan clubs are still active into the twenty-first century. Some clubs even detail recent "Elvis sightings."

■ Elvis's stage presence made him a rock and roll superstar.

WORLD FOCUS

STAIRWAY TO STARDOM

The British band Led Zeppelin became an instant success in 1969. The group was famous for its screaming guitar solos and powerful vocals. It developed what became known as heavy metal rock. In 1971, the band's fame shot through the roof with the release of "Stairway to Heaven." The eight-minute-long hit started out slowly but led into the band's signature thrashing electric guitar. To date, the record has sold around 10 million copies and continues to be voted the best song in music history. With other hits such as "Ramble On" and "Whole Lotta Love," Led Zeppelin claimed legend status. The band was inducted into the Rock and Roll Hall of Fame in 1996.

Just the Way He Is

Billy Joel released his first album, *Cold Spring Harbor*, in 1971. It was poorly promoted, and the recording was accidentally sped up during production, distorting Joel's voice. He returned to playing a piano in a hotel bar for six months before being noticed by record executives in 1973. Joel signed a contract with Columbia Records and recorded *Piano Man* (1973), *Streetlife Serenade* (1974), and *Turnstiles* (1976). A few of the songs on these albums, including "Piano Man," reached the Billboard top forty.

In 1977, Joel finally got the recognition he was seeking. His album *The Stranger* reached number two on the Billboard charts and contained a top-ten song, "Just the Way You Are." The single won two 1978 Grammy Awards and made Billy Joel a star. Many of Joel's songs, including "My Life" (1978) and "Uptown Girl" (1983), dominated U.S. radio. He continued to record music into the nineties. In 1991, he was awarded a Grammy Legends Award for his contribution to music.

■ Richard Nixon and Leonid Brezhnev toast the signing of the Space Flight Agreement in Moscow, May 26, 1972.

> "Let our goal now be a world without fear."
>
> President Nixon

No Stars and Stripes in Vietnam

On March 30, 1972, more than 30,000 North Vietnamese troops crossed the neutral zone and attacked Quang Ti Province in South Vietnam. In response to this attack, President Nixon ordered a bombing campaign against North Vietnamese troops. Nixon continued the offensive for seven months, after which at least 100,000 communist troops lay dead. Talks were set up to bring an end to the fighting.

An end to America's longest war was in sight. U.S. Secretary of State, Henry Kissinger, and Le Duc Tho, the North Vietnam representative, agreed to a ceasefire and withdrawal, but South Vietnam's Nguyen van Thieu was not happy. He accused the U.S. of selling out his country. Nixon refused to sign the agreement. After more bombings, both sides returned to the negotiations. On January 27, 1973, the Vietnam War ended with the signing of the Treaty of Paris. By March 29, all U.S. troops were out of Vietnam. On paper the war was over, but fighting continued in Vietnam until 1975, when the North defeated the South.

New Comrades

Richard Nixon became the first U.S. president to visit the USSR. In 1972, Nixon met with the Soviet leader, Leonid Brezhnev, in Moscow. The meeting was a great success. The two leaders discussed trade, arms control, and scientific cooperation. The most noteworthy agreements to come of the visit were the treaties known as SALT I and SALT II, in which Nixon and Brezhnev agreed to limit the number of their missiles and nuclear weapons. They also discussed having joint projects in space. This came about in 1975, with the *Apollo-Soyuz* space docking. While some Americans were skeptical of the new friendship, many were thankful that the Cold War was thawing.

EAST WARMS UP

■ After twenty years of disagreeing with each other, the People's Republic of China and the U.S. came together. President Nixon began to repair a strained relationship between China and the U.S. on June 10, 1971, when he announced that he would drop the decades-old trade embargo against China. Then on February 21, 1972, Nixon became the first U.S. president to meet with Chinese communists. President Nixon and Secretary of State Henry Kissinger met with Chinese Premier Zhou Enlai and Chairman Mao Zedong to discuss issues, including the threat of the Soviet Union. The trip did not accomplish much in the way of trade agreements, but the leaders promised to join together to work toward world peace.

CIA Assassins

In the 1970s, it was alleged that the Central Intelligence Agency (CIA) was linked to assassinations and the coup in Chile. The U.S. reportedly spent $13.5 million to get the Chilean president, Salvador Allende, out of office. The agency financed an anti-Allende newspaper and was said to have encouraged the 1973 coup in which Allende was killed. There were additional reports that the CIA had plotted to kill Premier Patrice Lumumba of Zaire and Fidel Castro of Cuba. It was also suggested that the agency encouraged or knew about coups that killed Vietnamese President Ngo Dinh Diem, Chilean General Rene Schneider, and dictator Rafael Trujillo of the Dominican Republic. Frank Church's Senate panel revealed these events in a report. As a result of these accusations, the government established permanent committees to watch over CIA operations.

■ Both Castro and Allende were targets of CIA operations.

Held Hostage

In 1979, 500 Iranian students backed by Ayatollah Khomeini, Iran's religious leader, invaded the U.S. Embassy in Tehran, Iran. They took ninety hostages. The revolutionaries were angry that the U.S. had allowed the **Shah** of Iran to have surgery in American hospitals. President Carter froze all Iranian assets in U.S. banks and sent a task force to the Indian Ocean so that it would be within attacking distance of Iran. Horrified Americans watched as blindfolded marines appeared on television with their hands bound. Around them, Iranians chanted "Death to America! Death to the Shah!" The terrorists demanded that the Shah be sent back to them.

Carter tried to negotiate but had little success. A few hostages, mostly women and African Americans, were released, leaving fifty-two captives. An evacuation was attempted, but it failed, and eight people were killed. The remaining hostages were released on January 20, 1981.

Where Did It Happen?

Match each number with an event.

a) The first assassination attempt on President Ford
b) Watergate break-in
c) Kent State University shooting
d) Nuclear meltdown
e) Sears Tower built

f) Undefeated season for a football team
g) Hank Aaron joins a professional team
h) Mission control saves a shuttle
i) Love Canal trouble
j) Pipeline's end point

Hawai'ian Islands

Answers: 1. i); 2. b); 3. a); 4. d); 5. h); 6. f); 7. j); 8. e); 9. c); 10. g).

True or False

1. William Styron wrote the book *Roots* which was made into a successful television miniseries.

2. New York city was close to going bankrupt.

3. Bobby Riggs beat Billie Jean King in a tennis match.

4. General Pinochet won the election against President Allende.

5. Americans were first able to videotape television programs in the seventies.

Answers:
1. False (*Roots* was written by Alex Haley)
2. True
3. False (King beat him)
4. False (There was no election. Pinochet took the government in a coup)
5. True

Newsmakers

Match the 1970s newsmakers with their claim to fame.

1. created a Pulitzer Prize-winning comic strip

2. tried to assassinate President Ford

3. author of *Roots*

4. astronaut on *Apollo 13* mission

5. beat Babe Ruth's home-run record

6. starred as a mafia boss

7. went to prison for writing a book

8. won two Grammy Awards in 1978

9. Egyptian leader who negotiated peace

10. involved in the Watergate scandal

a) Marlon Brando
b) G. Gordon Liddy
c) Anwar al-Sadat
d) Clifford Irving
e) Billy Joel
f) Garretsom Trudeau
g) Hank Aaron
h) John L. Swigert
i) Lynette Fromme
j) Alex Haley

Answers: 1 f); 2 i); 3 j); 4 h); 5 g); 6 a) ; 7 d); 8 e); 9 c); 10 b).

anti-hero: a central character in a story who lacks the usual heroic qualities

censored: restricted and controlled what could be written

cerebral edema: a burst blood vessel in the brain

commune: a group of people who are not all from the same family but who share accommodation and goods

coup: an often violent overthrow of a government

cults: religious groups with unusual or extreme customs

decision: a judges ruling on the winner of a boxing match

default: fail to pay back a loan

defected: escaped from one's country in order to live in another

eavesdropping: listening in on a private conversation

embargo: stoppage of trade and other commercial activities

enlist: sign up

enthralled: interested, captivated

feminists: supporters of the claim to women's equal rights

gene: factor in the body that controls heredity

genetic engineering: altering genetic material to change heredity characteristics

guerrillas: paramilitary soldiers, usually with a political objective such as the overthrow of a government

impeachment: being charged with an offense as a public official

integrated: brought together in equal membership

lobotomized: having had an incision in the frontal lobe of the brain; it alters the individual's personality

mafia: organized group of criminals originally from Italy

Manson family: a religious group led by Charles Manson in the sixties

meltdown: the melting of and damage to a nuclear reactor

mutations: changes or alterations to a gene

oppressed: governed harshly and treated with cruelty

persecution: cruel treatment often because of religion or political beliefs

prequel: the story that came before events

prestigious: bringing respect or a good reputation

Pulitzer Prize: money prizes given in journalism, literature, music, and history

recluse: a person who lives alone and does not associate much with other people

segregation: separating one racial group from another

Shah: ruler of Iran

subpoenas: orders that command people to appear in a law court to testify

trilogy: a group of three related works

vigil: a time spent in prayer or reflection

Here are some book resources and Internet links if you want to learn more about the people, places, and events that made headlines during the 1970s.

Books

Anderson, Christopher. *The Book of People*. New York: G.P. Putnam's Sons, 1981.

Brewster, Todd and Peter Jennings. *The Century for Young People*. New York: Random House Inc., 1999.

Lawson, Don. *The War in Vietnam*. New York: F. Watts, 1981.

Ward, Ed, Geoffrey Stokes, and Ken Tucker. *Rock of Ages: The Rolling Stone History of Rock & Roll*. New York: Rolling Stone Press, 1986.

The 20th Century Year By Year. Vancouver: New Millennium Books, 1999.

Internet Links

http://www.kconline.com/kurtkelsey/retro

http://www.bbhq.com/seventez.htm

http://www.cnn.com/allpolitics/1997/gen/resources/watergate

www.geocities.com/sunsetstrip/8678

For information about other U.S. subjects, type your key words into a search engine such as Alta Vista or Yahoo!